NAIL SALON STARTUP GUIDE

A Comprehensive Guide to Starting, Running and Growing a Successful Beauty Salon

CHERYL CALDWELL

Copyright Notice

This book is copyrighted in 2019-2022 by Dan & Elbert Associates.

All rights reserved.
Its content may not be copied or duplicated in part or whole by any means without express prior agreement in writing

TABLE OF CONTENTS

Introduction	5
Chapter 1: Introduction to the Nail Salon Industry	7
Understanding the Beauty Industry Landscape	7
Trends and Opportunities in Nail Care	9
Why Start a Nail Salon?	10
Chapter 2: Crafting Your Vision	13
Defining Your Unique Selling Proposition	13
Identifying Your Target Market	15
Creating Your Brand Identity	17
Chapter 3: Developing a Business Plan	19
Market Research and Analysis	19
Setting Goals and Objectives	21
Financial Planning and Budgeting	22
Chapter 4: Legal and Regulatory Considerations	25
Choosing a Business Structure	25
Obtaining Licenses and Permits	26
Compliance with Health and Safety Regulations	27
Chapter 5: Location, Location, Location	31
Finding the Perfect Location for Your Nail Salon	31
Lease Negotiation Tips	33
Designing Your Salon Space	35
Chapter 6: Nail Salon Essentials	39
Equipment and Supplies Checklist	39
Selecting Nail Products and Brands	41

    Creating a Comfortable and Hygienic Environment   42

Chapter 7: Building Your Team   **47**

    Hiring Qualified Nail Technicians   47

    Training and Development   49

    Cultivating a Positive Work Culture   50

Chapter 8: Marketing and Promotion   **53**

    Developing a Marketing Strategy   53

    Building an Online Presence   57

    Implementing Promotional Tactics   58

Chapter 9: Managing Operations Efficiently   **61**

    Scheduling and Appointment Management   61

    Inventory Control and Product Management   62

    Bookkeeping and Financial Management   64

Chapter 10: Navigating Challenges and Overcoming Obstacles   **67**

    Common Challenges Faced by Nail Salon Owners   67

    Strategies for Problem-Solving and Conflict Resolution   69

    Maintaining Resilience and Persistence   71

Chapter 11: Growing Your Nail Salon Business   **75**

    Expanding Your Services and Offerings   75

    Increasing Revenue Streams   77

    Scaling Your Business for Long-Term Success   79

Conclusion   **83**

Introduction

Starting a nail salon can be an incredibly profitable venture in today's beauty industry landscape. With a growing demand for nail care services driven by increasing beauty consciousness and the desire for self-expression, nail salons offer a lucrative opportunity for entrepreneurs. As individuals seek to enhance their appearance and express their creativity through their fingertips, the demand for manicures, pedicures, nail art, and other nail care services continues to rise.

This book, "Nail Salon Startup Guide " is a comprehensive handbook for embarking on the exciting journey of starting and running your own nail salon business. Whether you're a seasoned nail technician looking to branch out on your own or someone with a passion for beauty and entrepreneurship, this book is your roadmap to success in the thriving world of nail care.

In recent years, the beauty industry, particularly the nail care sector, has witnessed remarkable growth and transformation. Nails are no longer just a grooming necessity; they have become a canvas for self-expression, creativity, and personal style. As more individuals seek professional nail services to enhance their look and pamper themselves, the demand for high-quality nail salons continues to soar.

However, diving into the world of entrepreneurship, especially in a competitive industry like beauty, can be daunting. From navigating legal regulations to finding the perfect location, from sourcing the right products to building a loyal clientele – there are numerous challenges and considerations involved in launching and running a successful nail salon.

That's where this book comes in. Drawing on years of industry experience, expert insights, and real-world examples, "Nail Salon Startup Guide" is designed to be your go-to resource for every step of the entrepreneurial journey. Whether you're in the early stages of brainstorming your business idea or you've already secured a location and are eager to get started, each chapter is packed with practical advice, actionable tips, and invaluable wisdom to help you turn your dream of owning a thriving nail salon into reality.

Throughout these pages, you'll learn how to craft a compelling vision for your salon, develop a solid business plan, navigate legal and regulatory requirements, design an inviting salon space, attract and retain talented staff, effectively market your services, provide exceptional customer experiences, and manage day-to-day operations efficiently. Additionally, you'll gain insights into overcoming challenges, adapting to industry trends, and positioning your salon for long-term success.

Whether your goal is to open a cozy boutique nail studio in your local neighborhood or launch a full-service spa catering to luxury clientele, this book provides the tools, strategies, and inspiration you need to make it happen. Each chapter is designed to empower you with the knowledge and confidence to overcome obstacles, seize opportunities, and build a thriving nail salon business that not only reflects your passion for beauty but also generates sustainable profits.

So, are you ready to embark on this exhilarating journey? It does not matter if you're a seasoned entrepreneur or a newcomer to the beauty industry, "Nail Salon Startup Guide" is your trusted companion on the path to turning your passion for nails into a profitable and fulfilling business venture. Let's begin this exciting adventure together!

Chapter 1:
Introduction to the Nail Salon Industry

In the vast and dynamic landscape of the beauty industry, nail care stands out as a vibrant and ever-evolving sector. From simple manicures to intricate nail art, the demand for professional nail services continues to rise, fueled by changing fashion trends, cultural influences, and evolving consumer preferences. In this chapter, we'll delve deep into the nail salon industry, exploring its growth trajectory, emerging trends, and the compelling reasons why aspiring entrepreneurs should consider starting their own nail salon.

Understanding the Beauty Industry Landscape

The beauty industry is a vast and diverse landscape, encompassing a wide array of products and services aimed at enhancing one's appearance and well-being. From skincare and haircare to makeup and fragrance, beauty enthusiasts have an abundance of options to choose from, each catering to different needs and preferences. Within this expansive industry, nail care stands out as a unique and dynamic segment, offering individuals the opportunity to express their creativity and style through their fingertips.

Nail care has a long and rich history, dating back thousands of years to ancient civilizations where people adorned their nails with natural dyes and pigments. Over time, nail care evolved from a simple grooming ritual to a form of self-expression and artistry. Today, nail salons offer a wide range of services, from basic manicures and pedicures to more elaborate treatments such as gel nails, acrylic nails, nail extensions, and intricate nail designs.

The popularity of nail care services has surged in recent years, driven by various factors contributing to the overall growth of the beauty industry. One of the primary drivers of growth is increasing disposable income, particularly in emerging markets where rising middle-class populations have greater spending power. As individuals have more discretionary income to spend on luxury and self-care products and services, the demand for nail care services has experienced a corresponding increase.

Furthermore, there has been a notable shift in beauty consciousness, with more people placing greater importance on grooming and personal appearance. In today's image-conscious society, nails have become a focal point of attention, with individuals seeking to achieve perfectly manicured and stylish nails that complement their overall look. The desire to project a polished and put-together appearance has fueled the demand for professional nail services, driving growth in the nail care segment.

Additionally, the influence of social media has played a significant role in shaping trends and driving consumer behavior within the beauty industry, including nail care. Platforms like Instagram, Pinterest, and TikTok have become hubs for beauty inspiration, where users share photos and videos of their latest nail designs, showcasing innovative techniques and creative nail art. As a result, consumers are increasingly exposed to a wide range of nail trends and styles, fueling their desire to experiment with different nail looks and seek out professional nail services to achieve their desired aesthetic.

According to market research firm Euromonitor International, the global beauty and personal care market surpassed $500 billion in 2020, with continued growth projected in the coming years. Within this thriving industry, the nail care segment has emerged as a particularly lucrative niche, offering ample opportunities for entrepreneurs and beauty professionals alike to capitalize on the growing demand for professional nail services.

The beauty industry is a dynamic and fast-growing sector, driven by factors such as increasing disposable income, rising beauty consciousness, and the influence of social media. Within this industry, nail care holds a unique position, offering individuals the opportunity to express their creativity and style through their fingertips. As the demand for professional nail services continues to rise, the nail care segment presents exciting opportunities for growth and innovation, making it an attractive niche for entrepreneurs and beauty enthusiasts alike.

Trends and Opportunities in Nail Care

In recent years, several trends have shaped the nail care industry, influencing consumer preferences and driving innovation. One of the most notable trends is the growing popularity of nail art. What was once considered a niche trend confined to fashion runways and celebrity circles has now become mainstream, thanks to social media platforms like Instagram and Pinterest, where users share photos of their elaborate nail designs, inspiring others to experiment with their own nails.

Another significant trend is the demand for natural and eco-friendly nail products. As consumers become more mindful of the ingredients used in their beauty products, there is a growing preference for non-toxic, vegan, and cruelty-free nail polishes and treatments. Nail salons that prioritize sustainability and environmental responsibility are well-positioned to attract eco-conscious clientele.

Furthermore, the rise of nail care subscription services and mobile nail technicians has transformed the way people access nail services. Busy professionals and individuals with hectic schedules appreciate the convenience of having nail treatments delivered to their doorstep or booking appointments at their preferred location.

Additionally, the COVID-19 pandemic has had a profound impact on the nail salon industry, prompting salon owners to implement strict hygiene protocols and adapt their services to ensure the safety of their clients and staff. As the world navigates the aftermath of the pandemic, there is an increased emphasis on cleanliness, sanitation, and contactless service delivery in nail salons.

Why Start a Nail Salon?

Amidst the evolving landscape of the beauty industry, starting a nail salon presents a compelling opportunity for aspiring entrepreneurs. Here are several reasons why venturing into the nail salon business can be a rewarding endeavor:

1. Growing Demand: The demand for professional nail services continues to rise, driven by factors such as changing fashion trends, increased beauty consciousness, and the desire for self-expression. As more individuals seek out nail treatments to enhance their appearance and express their personal style, there is ample opportunity for nail salon owners to attract a steady stream of clientele.

2. Creative Expression: Running a nail salon allows individuals with a passion for beauty and creativity to unleash their artistic talents. From creating intricate nail designs to experimenting with new techniques and trends, nail technicians have the opportunity to express themselves and showcase their skills through their work.

3. Lucrative Business Potential: The nail salon industry is known for its profitability, with high margins and low overhead costs compared to other businesses in the beauty sector. With the right combination of quality services, effective marketing, and exceptional customer service, nail salon owners can generate substantial revenue and achieve healthy profit margins.

4. Flexibility and Independence: For individuals seeking a flexible career path or the freedom to be their own boss, owning a nail salon offers the autonomy and independence they desire. Whether you choose to operate a small boutique salon or expand into a multi-location chain, the flexibility of entrepreneurship allows you to tailor your business to suit your lifestyle and goals.

5. Fulfilling Client Relationships: Building strong relationships with clients is one of the most rewarding aspects of running a nail salon. As a nail technician, you have the opportunity to make a positive impact on your clients' lives, boosting their confidence and helping them feel beautiful and pampered. The satisfaction of providing exceptional service and seeing the joy on your clients' faces is priceless.

In summary, the nail salon industry presents a wealth of opportunities for aspiring entrepreneurs seeking to combine their passion for beauty with the excitement of business ownership. From tapping into emerging trends to providing exceptional service and fostering meaningful client relationships, the journey of starting and running a nail salon is both fulfilling and financially rewarding. In the chapters that follow, we'll delve deeper into the essential steps and strategies for launching and growing a successful nail salon business, empowering you to turn your dreams into reality.

12

Chapter 2:
Crafting Your Vision

In the journey of starting a nail salon, crafting a clear and compelling vision is essential for laying the foundation of your business. This chapter focuses on the pivotal steps of defining your unique selling proposition, identifying your target market, and creating a brand identity that sets your nail salon apart from the competition.

Defining Your Unique Selling Proposition

Your unique selling proposition (USP) serves as the cornerstone of your nail salon's branding and marketing strategy. It defines what makes your salon stand out in a crowded marketplace and communicates the specific benefits and value proposition you offer to your customers. To define your USP effectively, consider the following steps:

1. Conduct a Competitive Analysis: Start by researching existing nail salons in your area to understand their strengths, weaknesses, and market positioning. Analyze factors such as services offered, pricing, quality of treatments, customer experience, and brand reputation. Identify gaps or areas where competitors may be underserving customers, as these can serve as opportunities for differentiation.

2. Identify Your Unique Attributes: Reflect on what sets your nail salon apart from others and how you can leverage these unique attributes to attract and retain customers. Consider factors such as specialized skills or expertise, innovative nail techniques, use of high-quality and eco-friendly products, personalized customer service, or a distinctive salon ambiance. Think about what aspects of your salon resonate most with your target market and differentiate you from competitors.

3. Highlight Key Benefits: Once you've identified your unique attributes, clearly articulate the key benefits they offer to your customers. Whether it's flawless nail art, long-lasting treatments, a relaxing spa-like experience, or personalized consultations, emphasize how these benefits address the specific needs and preferences of your target audience. Your USP should clearly communicate the value customers can expect when choosing your nail salon over others.

4. Align with Your Target Market: Ensure that your USP resonates with your target market and aligns with their preferences, lifestyle, and values. Consider the demographic, psychographic, and behavioral characteristics of your ideal customers, and tailor your USP to address their unique needs and desires. By understanding your target market and speaking directly to their concerns and aspirations, you can create a more compelling and relevant USP.

5. Communicate Your USP Effectively: Once you've defined your USP, integrate it into your branding, marketing, and customer communications. Incorporate your USP into your salon's name, logo, tagline, website, social media profiles, and promotional materials. Use storytelling and visual imagery to bring your USP to life and create a memorable brand experience that resonates with customers.

Remember that your USP is not set in stone and may evolve over time as your salon grows and adapts to changing market dynamics. Continuously monitor industry trends, customer feedback, and competitive developments to ensure that your USP remains relevant and differentiated. By defining a strong and compelling USP, you can position your nail salon for success and attract a loyal customer base that values the unique benefits you offer.

Identifying Your Target Market

Understanding your target market is indeed essential for the success of your nail salon business. By gaining insights into the demographic, psychographic, and behavioral characteristics of your ideal customers, you can tailor your services, marketing efforts, and overall business strategy to effectively meet their needs and preferences. Here's a detailed guide on how to identify and understand your target market:

1. Conduct Market Research: Start by gathering data on your target market through market research. Identify key demographic factors such as age, gender, income level, occupation, and geographic location. This information will help you understand the basic characteristics of your target audience and segment them accordingly.

2. Explore Psychographic Factors: Dive deeper into the psychographic factors that influence your target audience's behavior and preferences. Consider aspects such as lifestyle, values, interests, hobbies, aspirations, and purchasing behavior. Understanding these psychographic insights will provide a more nuanced understanding of your customers and help you tailor your services and marketing messages accordingly.

3. Gather Customer Feedback: Conduct surveys, interviews, or focus groups with potential customers to gather feedback and insights into their needs, preferences, and pain points related to nail care services. Ask about their current nail care routines, favorite nail trends, preferences for salon ambiance, and desired level of customer service. This direct feedback will provide valuable insights into how you can position your nail salon to meet their expectations effectively.

4. Segment Your Target Market: Based on the data collected, segment your target market into distinct customer personas or segments. Group individuals with similar characteristics and preferences together to create detailed customer profiles. For example, you may have personas such as "Busy Professionals," "Fashion-forward Millennials," "Eco-conscious Consumers," or "Luxury Spa Enthusiasts." Each persona represents a specific segment of your target market with unique needs and preferences.

5. Tailor Your Services and Marketing Efforts: Once you have identified your target market segments, tailor your nail salon's services, marketing messages, and brand experience to resonate with each segment effectively. Customize your service offerings, pricing strategies, and promotional campaigns to address the specific needs and preferences of each customer persona. For example, you may offer express manicure services for busy professionals, trendy nail art designs for fashion-forward millennials, or organic nail treatments for eco-conscious consumers.

6. Monitor and Adapt: Continuously monitor market trends, customer feedback, and competitive developments to stay informed about changes in your target market. Be prepared to adapt your strategies and offerings accordingly to ensure that your nail salon remains relevant and competitive in the evolving beauty industry landscape.

By understanding your target market and tailoring your nail salon's services and marketing efforts accordingly, you can attract and retain loyal customers who resonate with your brand and value proposition. Investing time and resources into market research and segmentation will ultimately pay off in the form of increased customer satisfaction, loyalty, and business success.

Creating Your Brand Identity

Your brand identity is the visual and conceptual representation of your nail salon's personality, values, and unique attributes. It encompasses elements such as your salon name, logo, color scheme, typography, imagery, and overall aesthetic, all of which work together to convey a cohesive and memorable brand image.

When creating your brand identity, consider the following key elements:

1. Salon Name: Choose a name that reflects your salon's personality, values, and positioning in the market. Make sure it's easy to pronounce, spell, and remember, and conduct a thorough search to ensure the name is not already in use by another business.

2. Logo Design: Design a distinctive and visually appealing logo that captures the essence of your nail salon and resonates with your target audience. Consider incorporating elements such as nails, nail polish bottles, or artistic motifs that reflect your brand identity and differentiate your salon from competitors.

3. Color Scheme: Select a color palette that reflects the mood, atmosphere, and personality of your nail salon. Consider the psychological associations of different colors and choose hues that evoke the desired emotions and perceptions among your target audience.

4. Typography: Choose fonts that are legible, aesthetically pleasing, and consistent with your brand personality. Whether you opt for elegant scripts, modern sans-serifs, or playful hand-lettering, ensure that the typography reinforces your brand identity and aligns with your overall visual aesthetic.

5. Imagery: Curate a collection of images that showcase your nail salon's services, ambiance, and clientele. Invest in professional photography or create visually engaging content that highlights the expertise of your nail technicians, the quality of your nail treatments, and the inviting atmosphere of your salon.

By defining your unique selling proposition, identifying your target market, and creating a cohesive brand identity, you lay the groundwork for building a strong and distinctive presence in the competitive nail salon industry. In the chapters that follow, we'll delve deeper into the strategic planning and execution of your vision, empowering you to bring your dream nail salon to life and attract loyal customers who resonate with your brand.

Chapter 3:
Developing a Business Plan

A well-crafted business plan is the blueprint for success in starting and running a nail salon. In this chapter, we'll delve into the essential components of developing a comprehensive business plan, including conducting market research and analysis, setting clear goals and objectives, and creating a robust financial plan to ensure the financial viability and sustainability of your nail salon venture.

Market Research and Analysis

Market research is indeed a fundamental step in the process of developing a business plan for your nail salon. By gathering and analyzing relevant data about the beauty industry, local market conditions, customer demographics, and competitive landscape, you can gain valuable insights that will inform your business strategy and decision-making process.

To begin your market research, it's essential to understand the broader context of the beauty industry, with a specific focus on the nail care segment. This involves examining the size, growth potential, and dynamics of the beauty industry as a whole, as well as the specific trends and opportunities within the nail care sector. Industry reports, market studies, and trade publications are valuable resources for gathering information about industry trends, consumer preferences, and emerging opportunities. These sources can provide insights into factors such as popular nail styles, preferred nail care products, and evolving consumer behaviors.

Once you have a grasp of the broader industry landscape, the next step is to assess the local market conditions in your area. Understanding the demographic and economic characteristics of your target market is crucial for identifying opportunities and challenges specific to your geographical location. Analyze factors such as population demographics, income levels, spending habits, and lifestyle preferences to gain a deeper understanding of your potential customer base. Additionally, consider local market trends, such as seasonal fluctuations in demand for nail services, to tailor your business strategy accordingly.

Conducting primary research, such as surveys, interviews, or focus groups with potential customers, can provide invaluable insights into their nail care needs and preferences. By engaging directly with your target market, you can gather feedback on topics such as preferred nail styles, desired salon amenities, pricing sensitivity, and satisfaction with existing nail salons in the area. This qualitative data can complement quantitative market research and provide a more comprehensive understanding of your target market's needs and preferences.

Furthermore, it's essential to conduct a thorough analysis of the competitive landscape to identify existing nail salons in your area and understand their strengths and weaknesses. This competitive analysis involves researching factors such as pricing strategies, service offerings, salon ambiance, customer service, and marketing tactics. By understanding the competitive landscape, you can identify gaps or areas where you can differentiate your nail salon and capitalize on unmet customer needs. For example, if existing nail salons in your area primarily offer basic manicure and pedicure services, there may be an opportunity to differentiate your salon by specializing in niche services such as nail art, gel extensions, or organic nail treatments.

In summary, market research is a critical first step in developing a business plan for your nail salon. By gathering and analyzing relevant data about the beauty industry, local market conditions, customer demographics, and competitive landscape, you can gain valuable insights that will inform your business strategy and decision-making process. Whether you're assessing industry trends, understanding your target market, or analyzing the competitive landscape, market research provides the foundation for a successful nail salon business.

Setting Goals and Objectives

Setting clear and measurable goals and objectives is essential for guiding the direction and focus of your nail salon business. Goals provide a roadmap for what you want to achieve, while objectives outline specific actions and milestones to reach those goals. When setting goals and objectives for your nail salon, consider the following:

1. Business Mission and Vision: Start by defining your nail salon's mission and vision statements, which articulate the purpose and long-term aspirations of your business. Your mission statement should succinctly describe what your nail salon does and why it exists, while your vision statement outlines your ultimate goals and aspirations for the future.

2. Short-term and Long-term Goals: Identify both short-term and long-term goals for your nail salon, taking into account factors such as revenue targets, customer acquisition goals, expansion plans, and brand building initiatives. Short-term goals may include launching your salon, attracting your first clients, and achieving profitability within the first year, while long-term goals may involve expanding into new locations, diversifying your service offerings, or becoming a market leader in your area.

3. SMART Objectives: Ensure that your goals and objectives are SMART – specific, measurable, achievable, relevant, and time-bound. For example, rather than setting a vague goal like "increase revenue," set a specific objective such as "increase monthly

revenue by 20% within the next six months by implementing targeted marketing campaigns and promotions."

4. Key Performance Indicators (KPIs): Identify key performance indicators (KPIs) to track your progress towards achieving your goals and objectives. Examples of KPIs for a nail salon may include customer retention rates, average ticket size, appointment booking rates, client satisfaction scores, and revenue per service.

5. Flexibility and Adaptability: While it's important to set ambitious goals and objectives for your nail salon, be prepared to adapt and adjust your plans as needed based on changing market conditions, customer feedback, and unforeseen challenges. Remain flexible and open to pivoting your strategy to stay aligned with your overarching business goals.

Financial Planning and Budgeting

Financial planning and budgeting are essential components of your nail salon business plan, ensuring that you have a clear understanding of your startup costs, operating expenses, revenue projections, and profitability expectations. A well-developed financial plan will help you make informed decisions, secure financing, and manage your finances effectively.

Start by estimating your startup costs, which may include expenses such as leasehold improvements, equipment purchases, inventory, marketing materials, salon furnishings, licensing fees, and initial working capital. Create a detailed budget that outlines each expense category and estimates the associated costs, allowing for contingencies and unexpected expenses.

Next, project your revenue potential by forecasting sales for each of your nail salon services based on factors such as pricing, market demand, and anticipated customer volume. Consider conducting market research and benchmarking against industry standards to ensure that your revenue projections are realistic and achievable.

Once you have estimated your startup costs and revenue projections, create a financial forecast that outlines your expected cash flow, profit and loss statement, and balance sheet for the first year of operation. This financial forecast will help you assess the financial viability of your nail salon business and identify any potential cash flow challenges or areas for improvement.

In addition to your initial startup costs and revenue projections, consider ongoing operating expenses such as rent, utilities, insurance, payroll, supplies, marketing, and maintenance. Develop a monthly or quarterly budget that outlines your expected expenses and revenue targets, allowing you to track your financial performance and make adjustments as needed to stay on track towards your financial goals.

Finally, consider your financing options for funding your nail salon startup. Explore sources of funding such as personal savings, loans, grants, investors, or crowdfunding, and determine the most appropriate financing strategy based on your financial needs and risk tolerance.

In summary, developing a comprehensive business plan for your nail salon involves conducting thorough market research and analysis, setting clear goals and objectives, and creating a robust financial plan to ensure the financial viability and success of your business venture. By investing time and effort into developing a well-crafted business plan, you can lay the groundwork for a successful nail salon business and increase your chances of achieving your entrepreneurial goals.

Chapter 4:
Legal and Regulatory Considerations

Navigating the legal and regulatory landscape is essential when starting a nail salon business. In this chapter, we'll explore the key considerations, including choosing a business structure, obtaining licenses and permits, and ensuring compliance with health and safety regulations, to ensure your nail salon operates smoothly and legally.

Choosing a Business Structure

Selecting the right business structure is a crucial decision that will impact various aspects of your nail salon business, including taxes, liability, and operational flexibility. Here are some common business structures to consider:

1. Sole Proprietorship: A sole proprietorship is the simplest and most common form of business ownership, where a single individual owns and operates the business. In this structure, the owner is personally liable for all business debts and obligations.

2. Partnership: A partnership involves two or more individuals sharing ownership and management responsibilities of the business. Partnerships can be general partnerships, where all partners have equal rights and responsibilities, or limited partnerships, where one or more partners have limited liability.

3. Limited Liability Company (LLC): An LLC offers the liability protection of a corporation with the flexibility and tax benefits of a partnership. Owners of an LLC, known as members, are not personally liable for the company's debts and obligations, and the business's profits and losses pass through to the members' personal tax returns.

4. Corporation: A corporation is a separate legal entity that is owned by shareholders. Unlike sole proprietorships and partnerships, corporations provide limited liability protection to their owners, meaning shareholders are not personally liable for the company's debts and obligations. Corporations are subject to more complex legal and tax requirements.

When choosing a business structure for your nail salon, consider factors such as your risk tolerance, desired level of control, tax implications, and long-term growth plans. Consult with legal and financial professionals to determine the most appropriate structure for your specific circumstances.

Obtaining Licenses and Permits

Operating a nail salon requires obtaining various licenses and permits to ensure compliance with state and local regulations. The specific licenses and permits you'll need will depend on factors such as your location, business structure, and the services you offer. Here are some common licenses and permits required for nail salons:

1. Business License: Most jurisdictions require nail salons to obtain a general business license to operate legally within the area. This license typically covers basic business registration and may be obtained from the local government or municipal office.

2. Salon License: Some states require nail salons to obtain a specific salon license or permit to operate. This license may include requirements such as minimum education or training requirements for nail technicians, sanitation standards, and facility inspections.

3. Cosmetology License: Nail technicians must typically hold a cosmetology or nail technician license issued by the state licensing board. To obtain a cosmetology license, individuals must complete

a state-approved cosmetology or nail technician training program and pass a licensing exam.

4. Health Department Permit: Nail salons may be required to obtain a health department permit to ensure compliance with health and safety regulations, particularly regarding sanitation practices and infection control. Health department inspections may be conducted periodically to ensure compliance.

5. Zoning Permit: Before opening a nail salon, you may need to obtain a zoning permit to ensure that your business location complies with local zoning regulations. Zoning laws regulate the use of land and buildings and may restrict certain types of businesses in specific areas.

It's essential to research the licensing requirements in your area and ensure that you obtain all necessary licenses and permits before opening your nail salon. Failure to comply with regulatory requirements could result in fines, penalties, or even closure of your business.

Compliance with Health and Safety Regulations

Maintaining a safe and hygienic environment is paramount in the nail salon industry to protect the health and well-being of both clients and employees. Compliance with health and safety regulations is essential to prevent the spread of infections, allergic reactions, and other health risks associated with nail care services. Here are some key health and safety considerations for nail salons:

1. Sanitation Practices: Implement strict sanitation practices to ensure that all tools, equipment, and surfaces are properly cleaned, disinfected, and sterilized between each client. Use EPA-approved disinfectants and follow manufacturer guidelines for effective sanitation.

2. Ventilation Systems: Install adequate ventilation systems to ensure proper air circulation and reduce exposure to potentially harmful fumes and chemicals. Proper ventilation helps minimize respiratory irritation and improves air quality within the salon.

3. Personal Protective Equipment (PPE): Provide personal protective equipment, such as gloves and masks, to nail technicians to protect against exposure to hazardous chemicals and infectious agents. Encourage proper hand hygiene and frequent handwashing to prevent the spread of germs.

4. Chemical Safety: Follow proper protocols for handling and storing nail care products, including acrylics, gels, and polishes. Ensure that chemicals are labeled correctly, stored in appropriate containers, and used in well-ventilated areas to minimize exposure risks.

5. Education and Training: Provide comprehensive education and training to nail technicians on proper sanitation practices, infection control procedures, and chemical safety protocols. Regularly update training to ensure that staff remain knowledgeable about best practices and regulatory requirements.

6. Client Communication: Communicate with clients about the importance of health and safety practices and any precautions they should take before and after nail care services. Provide information about proper nail care hygiene and encourage clients to voice any concerns or questions they may have.

7. Regulatory Compliance: Stay informed about federal, state, and local health and safety regulations governing nail salon operations. Regularly review and update your policies and procedures to ensure compliance with current standards and best practices.

By prioritizing health and safety compliance in your nail salon, you can create a safe and welcoming environment for clients and

 employees alike. Implementing rigorous sanitation practices, providing ongoing education and training, and staying informed about regulatory requirements will help ensure the long-term success and sustainability of your nail salon business.

Chapter 5:
Location, Location, Location

The significance of the location cannot be overstated when it comes to starting a nail salon. Finding the perfect location can significantly impact your salon's success, visibility, and accessibility to potential clients. In this chapter, we will explore the critical aspects of finding the ideal location for your nail salon, negotiating lease terms effectively, and designing your salon space to create a welcoming and functional environment for both clients and staff.

Finding the Perfect Location for Your Nail Salon

When seeking the ideal location for your nail salon, several key factors should guide your decision-making process to ensure the success of your business venture. Firstly, understanding your target market demographics and preferences is paramount. By considering factors such as age, income level, lifestyle, and purchasing behavior, you can pinpoint locations that align with the needs and preferences of your desired clientele. Selecting a location that is easily accessible to your target market ensures convenience and encourages frequent visits.

Visibility and accessibility are crucial elements to prioritize when evaluating potential locations. Aim for a location with high visibility and easy accessibility to attract walk-in clients and drive-by traffic. Opting for a spot with ample signage opportunities and excellent visibility from the street increases your salon's visibility and catches the attention of potential customers passing by. This visibility can be a significant asset in drawing in new clients and increasing foot traffic to your salon.

Assessing the level of competition in the area is another critical consideration. While some competition can indicate a healthy market demand for nail services, excessive competition may pose challenges in standing out and attracting clients. Conduct a thorough analysis of the competitive landscape to identify gaps in the market or opportunities to offer unique services that differentiate your salon from competitors. By understanding the competition, you can tailor your offerings and marketing strategies to meet the needs of your target market effectively.

Safety and security should also be prioritized when selecting a location for your nail salon. Choose a location in a safe neighborhood with low crime rates and adequate lighting to ensure the well-being of both clients and staff. Prioritizing safety creates a sense of trust and comfort among clients, contributing to a positive salon experience and fostering long-term customer loyalty.

Consideration of amenities and infrastructure is essential for enhancing the overall client experience and attracting repeat business. Evaluate the availability of amenities such as parking facilities, public transportation options, shopping centers, restaurants, and other businesses in the area. Choosing a location with convenient amenities ensures ease of access for clients and enhances the overall appeal of your salon. Providing a seamless and convenient experience for clients encourages repeat visits and fosters positive word-of-mouth referrals.

Lastly, assess the long-term growth potential of the location and its impact on your salon's success. Research economic trends, development plans, and population growth projections to gauge the area's potential for future expansion and demand for nail salon services. Selecting a location with favorable growth prospects positions your salon for long-term success and sustainability in the competitive beauty industry landscape.

When searching for the perfect location for your nail salon, it's essential to consider factors such as target market demographics, visibility, competition, safety, amenities, and long-term growth potential. By carefully evaluating these factors and selecting a location that aligns with your business goals and target market preferences, you can set your nail salon up for success and attract a loyal clientele.

Lease Negotiation Tips

Once you've identified a potential location for your nail salon, the subsequent crucial step is negotiating a lease agreement with the property owner or landlord. Lease negotiation is a pivotal phase that can significantly impact your salon's profitability and long-term success. To ensure the negotiation of a favorable lease agreement, several key steps and considerations are imperative.

Firstly, it's essential to conduct due diligence on the property. This involves a comprehensive examination of various factors, including the property's history, zoning regulations, building codes, and existing lease terms. Understanding these aspects provides insight into any potential limitations or obligations associated with the property, allowing you to make informed decisions during the negotiation process.

Seeking assistance from a real estate attorney or leasing agent with expertise in commercial real estate transactions is highly recommended. These professionals can provide invaluable guidance and support throughout the lease negotiation process. They can review lease terms, identify potential pitfalls, and advocate for your interests to ensure the negotiation of favorable terms that align with your salon's needs and goals.

Understanding common lease terms and clauses is essential for navigating the negotiation process effectively. Key terms to consider include rent, lease duration, renewal options, maintenance responsibilities, utilities, and property improvements. Negotiating competitive rent rates and seeking to minimize additional expenses such as common area maintenance (CAM) fees, property taxes, insurance, and utilities can significantly impact your salon's financial viability.

Requesting rent concessions, tenant improvement allowances, or rent abatements can help offset initial startup costs and improve cash flow during the early stages of your salon's operation. These concessions provide financial flexibility and support your salon's growth and success in the competitive market.

Clarifying use restrictions and including provisions to protect your rights as a tenant are essential aspects of lease negotiation. Ensuring that the lease agreement addresses issues such as lease assignment, subleasing, lease termination, and dispute resolution protects your interests and provides recourse in case of disagreements or disputes with the landlord.

Before signing any lease documents, it's crucial to review them carefully and thoroughly. Ensure that the terms and conditions accurately reflect the negotiated agreements and seek clarification on any unclear or ambiguous provisions. By conducting a comprehensive review of all lease documents, you can mitigate the risk of misunderstandings or disputes down the line and secure a lease agreement that serves the best interests of your nail salon business.

In summary, lease negotiation is a critical step in establishing your nail salon business and securing a suitable location for its operation. By conducting due diligence, seeking professional assistance, understanding common lease terms, and clarifying rights and provisions, you can negotiate a favorable lease agreement that supports your salon's profitability, growth, and long-term success in the competitive beauty industry landscape.

Designing Your Salon Space

The design and layout of your salon space play a significant role in creating a welcoming and functional environment for clients and staff. Thoughtful salon design can enhance the client experience, improve workflow efficiency, and contribute to the overall success of your nail salon. When designing your salon space, prioritize layout and flow to optimize traffic flow and maximize space utilization. Designate separate areas for manicure and pedicure services, nail art stations, and drying stations to accommodate different client needs and preferences.

Creating a welcoming and inviting atmosphere is crucial for a nail salon to leave a lasting impression on clients and foster a sense of comfort and relaxation. The ambiance of a salon plays a significant role in shaping the overall customer experience and influencing client satisfaction and loyalty. To achieve this, it's essential to design a salon space that not only reflects your brand identity but also resonates with your target clientele.

One of the first considerations when designing the salon space is the color scheme. Colors have a profound impact on mood and perception, so choosing a cohesive color palette that aligns with your brand identity and evokes the desired atmosphere is key. Soft, muted tones such as pastel blues, greens, and neutrals can create a serene and calming environment, while brighter hues like pinks and oranges can add a touch of energy and vibrancy. Consider incorporating your brand colors into the decor to reinforce brand recognition and consistency.

Lighting is another crucial element that can significantly impact the ambiance of a salon. Natural light is ideal for creating a bright and airy atmosphere, so if possible, maximize the use of windows and skylights to bring in natural sunlight. Additionally, invest in ambient lighting fixtures such as overhead chandeliers, pendant lights, or wall sconces to create a warm and inviting glow. Task lighting is essential for nail technicians to ensure proper visibility during nail services, so provide ample task lighting at each nail station.

When selecting furniture and decor elements for the salon, prioritize comfort, functionality, and aesthetics. Choose ergonomic furniture that provides proper support and alignment for both technicians and clients during nail services. Comfortable chairs with cushioned seats and armrests can enhance the overall client experience and encourage relaxation. Opt for durable materials that are easy to clean and maintain, such as leather or vinyl upholstery.

Incorporate decorative elements that reflect your salon's brand identity and create a cohesive theme throughout the space. This could include artwork, wall decals, or branded signage that adds visual interest and personality to the salon. Consider incorporating natural elements such as potted plants or floral arrangements to bring a touch of nature indoors and create a fresh and inviting atmosphere.

Finally, pay attention to the layout and flow of the salon space to ensure a seamless and enjoyable experience for clients. Arrange furniture and nail stations in a way that maximizes space and allows for easy movement and accessibility. Create designated areas for different services, such as manicures, pedicures, and waiting areas, to ensure privacy and comfort for clients.

By focusing on creating a welcoming and inviting atmosphere that reflects your salon's brand identity and resonates with your target clientele, you can set the stage for a memorable and enjoyable nail salon experience. With thoughtful attention to detail and careful consideration of elements such as color, lighting, furniture, and decor, you can create a salon space that clients look forward to visiting time and time again.

Incorporate sanitation and safety measures into the salon design to ensure compliance with health and safety regulations. Install sinks with touchless faucets for handwashing, provide ample storage for clean and dirty implements, and implement strict protocols for disinfecting and sterilizing tools and surfaces between clients. Infuse your salon space with elements of your brand identity and branding to create a cohesive and memorable brand experience for clients.

Design your salon space with flexibility and adaptability in mind to accommodate changes in client preferences, seasonal trends, and business needs. Choose modular furniture and flexible layout configurations that can be easily reconfigured or repurposed as needed. By carefully planning and designing your salon space with these considerations in mind, you can create a welcoming, functional, and aesthetically pleasing environment that enhances the client experience and sets your nail salon apart from competitors.

Chapter 6:
Nail Salon Essentials

In this chapter, we delve into the fundamental aspects of setting up a nail salon, focusing on the essential equipment, supplies, products, and environment necessary to deliver high-quality nail care services. From selecting the right equipment and supplies to choosing the best nail products and brands, creating a comfortable and hygienic environment is paramount for the success and reputation of your nail salon.

Equipment and Supplies Checklist

To ensure smooth operations and exceptional service delivery in your nail salon, it's crucial to equip your salon with the necessary tools, equipment, and supplies. Here's a comprehensive checklist of essential items for your nail salon:

1. Nail Stations: Invest in high-quality nail stations equipped with comfortable seating, ergonomic nail tables, and adequate storage space for tools and supplies.

2. Manicure Tables: Provide manicure tables with built-in ventilation systems, task lighting, and storage compartments for manicure tools and products.

3. Pedicure Chairs: Choose pedicure chairs with adjustable settings, massage features, and built-in foot baths for a relaxing and comfortable pedicure experience.

4. Nail Care Tools: Stock up on essential nail care tools, including nail clippers, cuticle nippers, nail files, buffers, cuticle pushers, and tweezers.

5. Sanitation Supplies: Ensure proper sanitation practices by having ample supplies of disinfectants, sanitizers, disposable gloves, and disposable liners for pedicure foot baths.

6. UV/LED Nail Lamps: Invest in UV or LED nail lamps for curing gel polish and enhancing the durability of nail enhancements.

7. Air Filtration Systems: Install air filtration systems to minimize dust, fumes, and odors in the salon environment and maintain air quality for clients and technicians.

8. Salon Furniture: Choose comfortable and durable salon furniture, including reception desks, waiting area seating, retail display shelves, and employee breakroom furniture.

9. Nail Polish Display Racks: Organize and showcase your nail polish collection with stylish display racks that make it easy for clients to browse and select their favorite colors.

10. Towels and Linens: Stock up on clean towels, disposable towels, and disposable liners for pedicure tubs to maintain cleanliness and hygiene standards.

11. Nail Polish Remover: Provide acetone and non-acetone nail polish removers for safely removing nail polish without damaging the nails.

12. Hand and Foot Care Products: Offer a selection of hand creams, cuticle oils, foot scrubs, and moisturizers to pamper and nourish clients' hands and feet.

13. Nail Art Supplies: Keep a variety of nail art supplies on hand, including nail decals, stickers, rhinestones, glitter, and nail art brushes, to create unique and personalized nail designs.

14. Disposable Implements: Use disposable files, buffers, and orangewood sticks for single-use applications to maintain strict hygiene standards and prevent cross-contamination.

15. First Aid Kit: Keep a well-stocked first aid kit on hand to address minor injuries or accidents that may occur in the salon.

Selecting Nail Products and Brands

Choosing the right nail products and brands is essential for delivering high-quality nail care services and ensuring client satisfaction. Consider the following factors when selecting nail products and brands for your salon:

1. Quality: Prioritize quality when selecting nail products and brands to ensure optimal results and client satisfaction. Choose reputable brands known for their high-quality formulations, durability, and performance.

2. Variety: Offer a diverse range of nail products and brands to cater to different client preferences and nail care needs. Provide options for traditional polish, gel polish, dip powder, acrylics, and nail enhancements to accommodate a wide range of client preferences.

3. Safety: Ensure that nail products are formulated with safe and non-toxic ingredients to minimize the risk of allergic reactions, skin sensitivities, or other adverse effects. Choose products that are free from harmful chemicals such as formaldehyde, toluene, and dibutyl phthalate (DBP).

4. Trendiness: Stay updated on the latest nail trends and innovations in the beauty industry to offer trendy and fashionable nail products and designs. Provide seasonal color collections, new

product launches, and trendy nail art options to keep clients coming back for more.

5. Durability: Select nail products and brands known for their long-lasting durability and chip-resistant formulas. Clients appreciate nail services that maintain their beauty and integrity for extended periods, reducing the need for frequent touch-ups or repairs.

6. Compatibility: Ensure compatibility between different nail products and brands to achieve optimal results and avoid potential issues such as product lifting, chipping, or peeling. Test compatibility between base coats, top coats, and color products to ensure seamless application and adherence.

7. Training and Support: Choose nail product brands that offer comprehensive training programs, educational resources, and ongoing support for nail technicians. Access to training materials, product demonstrations, and technical support enhances nail technicians' skills and confidence in using the products effectively.

8. Client Feedback: Solicit feedback from clients on their preferences, experiences, and satisfaction with nail products and brands. Pay attention to client feedback and adjust your product offerings accordingly to meet their needs and preferences effectively.

Creating a Comfortable and Hygienic Environment

Creating a comfortable and hygienic environment is crucial for providing a safe, relaxing, and enjoyable experience for clients in your nail salon. Here are some essential tips for achieving this goal:

1. Cleanliness: Maintaining strict cleanliness and sanitation protocols throughout the salon is paramount. Implement a thorough cleaning schedule and checklist to ensure that all

surfaces, tools, and equipment are cleaned and disinfected regularly. Regular cleaning helps prevent the spread of germs and ensures a hygienic environment for both clients and staff.

2. Hygiene Practices: Proper hygiene practices are essential for safeguarding the health and well-being of everyone in the salon. Train nail technicians on the importance of handwashing, glove usage, and disinfection procedures. Encourage frequent handwashing and provide hand sanitizers for both clients and staff to promote good hygiene habits and minimize the risk of cross-contamination.

3. Ventilation: Adequate ventilation is essential for maintaining a comfortable and breathable environment in the salon. Ensure that the salon is well-ventilated to minimize dust, fumes, and odors. Consider installing air filtration systems or opening windows to improve air circulation and quality within the salon, creating a more pleasant atmosphere for clients and technicians alike.

4. Comfortable Seating: Invest in comfortable and ergonomic seating for both clients and technicians to enhance comfort during nail services. Choose chairs with adjustable settings, cushioned seats, and armrests to accommodate clients of all sizes and provide proper support during treatments. Comfortable seating contributes to a positive salon experience and encourages clients to relax and enjoy their services.

5. Relaxing Ambiance: Creating a relaxing and inviting ambiance in the salon helps clients unwind and enjoy their nail services to the fullest. Use soft lighting, soothing music, and calming decor elements to create a tranquil atmosphere. Consider using aromatherapy diffusers or scented candles to infuse the salon with pleasant aromas, further enhancing the overall client experience and promoting relaxation.

6. Privacy: Respect clients' privacy and personal space by providing designated treatment areas with adequate separation and privacy screens. Ensure that clients feel comfortable and relaxed during their nail services by minimizing distractions and maintaining a sense of privacy. Respecting clients' privacy enhances their comfort and allows them to fully enjoy their salon experience.

7. Client Comfort: Prioritize client comfort and satisfaction by offering amenities such as refreshments, magazines, and charging stations for electronic devices. Consider providing blankets or heated wraps during pedicure services to keep clients warm and cozy, especially during colder months. Going the extra mile to ensure client comfort enhances their overall salon experience and fosters loyalty.

8. Hygienic Practices: Implement strict hygienic practices to maintain a clean and sanitary salon environment. Ensure that all tools and equipment are properly cleaned and disinfected between clients to prevent the spread of infections. Use disposable liners for pedicure tubs and disposable implements for single-use applications to prevent cross-contamination and maintain strict hygiene standards. By prioritizing cleanliness and hygiene practices, you can create a safe and hygienic environment that instills confidence in clients and promotes their well-being.

By focusing on these essential aspects of nail salon essentials, you can create a comfortable, hygienic, and welcoming environment that promotes client satisfaction, loyalty, and repeat business. Prioritize quality, safety, and client comfort when selecting equipment, supplies, products, and brands for your salon, and implement strict cleanliness and hygiene practices to ensure the well-being of clients and staff alike. Creating a comfortable and hygienic salon environment sets the foundation for a successful and reputable nail salon business in the competitive beauty industry landscape.

Chapter 7:
Building Your Team

Building a talented and dedicated team of nail technicians is essential for the success and growth of your nail salon business. In this chapter, we will explore the key aspects of hiring, training, and cultivating a positive work culture within your salon.

Hiring Qualified Nail Technicians

Hiring qualified nail technicians is the cornerstone of building a strong team that can deliver exceptional service and uphold the reputation of your salon. Here's a detailed guide on how to hire the right candidates:

1. Define Job Roles and Responsibilities:

Start by clearly defining the roles and responsibilities of nail technicians within your salon. Determine the specific skills, qualifications, and experience required for each position, whether it's a manicurist, pedicurist, nail artist, or salon manager. Outline the duties and expectations associated with each role to ensure clarity during the hiring process.

2. Advertise Job Openings:

Advertise job openings through a variety of channels to attract qualified candidates. Utilize online job boards, social media platforms, industry associations, and local beauty schools to reach potential applicants. Craft engaging job descriptions that highlight the unique opportunities, benefits, and culture of your salon. Clearly communicate the requirements and qualifications necessary for the position to attract candidates who are the right fit for your salon.

3. Screen and Interview Candidates:

Screen resumes and applications to identify candidates who meet the basic qualifications and requirements for the position. Review candidates' education, experience, certifications, and relevant skills to assess their suitability for the role. Conduct initial phone screenings or video interviews to further evaluate candidates' communication skills, professionalism, and enthusiasm for the position. Select candidates who demonstrate a genuine passion for nail care and a strong commitment to providing exceptional service to clients.

4. Assess Portfolio and Work Samples:
Request portfolios or work samples from candidates to evaluate the quality of their nail artistry and technical skills. Review examples of their work to assess their creativity, attention to detail, and proficiency in various nail techniques. Look for candidates who demonstrate versatility and expertise in a range of services, such as gel nails, acrylics, nail extensions, and intricate designs. Consider the consistency and quality of their work when evaluating their suitability for the position.

5. Check References:
Contact references provided by candidates to verify their work history, skills, and character. Reach out to previous employers, colleagues, or clients to gain insights into candidates' performance, reliability, and professionalism. Ask specific questions about candidates' punctuality, work ethic, customer service skills, and ability to work well within a team. References can provide valuable information that helps you make informed hiring decisions and ensure that candidates align with your salon's values and standards.

6. Conduct Practical Assessments:
Consider conducting practical assessments or skills tests during the interview process to evaluate candidates' technical abilities in

real-world scenarios. Invite candidates to demonstrate their nail care skills by performing a mock manicure or pedicure, applying nail enhancements, or creating nail art designs. Observe their technique, precision, and attention to detail to assess their proficiency and suitability for the position. Practical assessments allow you to gauge candidates' hands-on abilities and ensure that they meet the standards of excellence expected by your salon.

By following these guidelines and investing time and effort in the hiring process, you can identify and hire qualified nail technicians who are skilled, professional, and passionate about delivering exceptional service to your clients. Building a talented and dedicated team lays the foundation for success and ensures that your salon continues to thrive in the competitive beauty industry landscape.

Training and Development

Once you've hired qualified nail technicians, invest in their training and development to ensure they have the skills and knowledge needed to excel in their roles. Here are some strategies for training and developing your team:

1. Provide Comprehensive Training: Offer comprehensive training programs to new hires that cover essential topics such as nail care techniques, sanitation and hygiene practices, customer service skills, product knowledge, and salon policies and procedures. Ensure that training is hands-on and interactive, allowing technicians to practice and refine their skills under the guidance of experienced mentors.

2. Offer Continuing Education Opportunities: Encourage ongoing learning and professional development by providing opportunities for continuing education and skills enhancement. Support technicians in attending workshops, seminars, trade shows, and

certification programs to stay updated on the latest trends, techniques, and industry best practices.

3. Foster Mentorship and Collaboration: Foster a culture of mentorship and collaboration within your salon, where experienced technicians can mentor and support newer team members. Encourage collaboration and knowledge sharing among team members, allowing them to learn from each other's experiences and expertise.

4. Provide Feedback and Recognition: Regularly provide feedback and recognition to your team members to acknowledge their accomplishments, identify areas for improvement, and motivate them to perform at their best. Recognize and celebrate individual achievements, milestones, and contributions to the success of the salon.

Cultivating a Positive Work Culture

Creating a positive work culture is essential for fostering teamwork, morale, and job satisfaction among your salon team. Here are some strategies for cultivating a positive work culture:

1. Lead by Example: As the salon owner or manager, lead by example and embody the values and principles you want to instill in your team. Demonstrate professionalism, respect, integrity, and a commitment to excellence in all your interactions and decisions.

2. Communicate Openly and Transparently: Foster open and transparent communication channels within your salon, where team members feel comfortable sharing feedback, ideas, and concerns. Encourage regular team meetings, one-on-one check-ins, and anonymous suggestion boxes to facilitate communication and address any issues promptly.

3. Recognize and Reward Achievement: Recognize and reward team members for their hard work, dedication, and contributions to the success of the salon. Implement a reward and recognition program that acknowledges outstanding performance, teamwork, and customer service excellence. Consider offering incentives such as bonuses, gift cards, or extra time off as tokens of appreciation.

4. Promote Work-Life Balance: Support work-life balance among your team members by offering flexible scheduling options, adequate time off, and support for personal wellness and self-care. Encourage employees to prioritize their physical and mental well-being, and lead by example by promoting a healthy work-life balance for yourself as well.

5. Foster a Supportive and Inclusive Environment: Create a supportive and inclusive work environment where team members feel valued, respected, and empowered to be their authentic selves. Embrace diversity and celebrate the unique backgrounds, perspectives, and talents of your team members. Address any instances of discrimination, harassment, or bullying promptly and ensure that all team members feel safe and welcome in the salon.

By hiring qualified nail technicians, investing in their training and development, and cultivating a positive work culture, you can build a talented and cohesive team that delivers exceptional service and drives the success of your nail salon business. Prioritize building strong relationships with your team members, and they will become your greatest asset in achieving your salon's goals and aspirations.

Chapter 8:
Marketing and Promotion

Marketing and promotion are essential components of building a successful nail salon business. In this chapter, we will explore the strategies and tactics necessary to attract and retain clients, increase brand awareness, and drive business growth.

Developing a Marketing Strategy

A well-defined marketing strategy is indeed the cornerstone of a successful nail salon business. It serves as a roadmap for attracting and retaining clients, increasing brand awareness, and ultimately driving revenue growth. Let's delve into the intricacies of developing a robust marketing strategy for your nail salon.

1. Identify Your Target Market:

   The first step in developing a marketing strategy is to identify your target market. Understand who your ideal clients are by conducting thorough market research. Gather insights into their demographics, including age, gender, income level, occupation, and geographic location. Additionally, delve into psychographic factors such as lifestyle, values, interests, and purchasing behavior. By understanding your target market's needs, preferences, and behaviors, you can tailor your marketing efforts more effectively to resonate with them.

2. Conduct Market Research:

   Market research is crucial for gaining insights into your target demographic and understanding the competitive landscape. Conduct surveys, interviews, or focus groups with potential clients to gather feedback and refine your understanding of their needs and preferences. Analyze industry reports, market studies, and competitor analysis to identify trends, opportunities, and gaps in the market.

3. Develop a Marketing Plan:

Based on your market research findings, develop a comprehensive marketing plan that outlines your salon's unique selling proposition (USP), positioning, and key messages. Define what sets your salon apart from competitors and articulate the value you offer to clients. Your marketing plan should also specify the marketing channels and tactics you will use to reach your target audience effectively. Consider a mix of traditional and digital marketing strategies to maximize your reach and effectiveness.

4. Determine Marketing Channels and Tactics:
Identifying the most effective marketing channels and tactics is crucial for reaching your target audience and driving business growth for your nail salon. By implementing a mix of both traditional and digital marketing strategies, you can maximize your reach and effectiveness in connecting with potential clients and increasing brand awareness. Let's explore some traditional and digital marketing tactics that can help you effectively promote your nail salon:

Traditional Marketing Tactics:

1. Print Advertising:
Placing advertisements in local newspapers, magazines, or community newsletters can help you reach a broad audience within your target geographic area. Print advertising allows you to showcase your salon's services, special promotions, and unique selling propositions to potential clients who may be interested in visiting your salon.

2. Direct Mail Campaigns:
Sending targeted mailers or postcards to residents in your salon's vicinity is an effective way to promote special offers, new services,

or upcoming events. Direct mail campaigns allow you to directly engage with potential clients in their homes and capture their attention with compelling visuals and messaging.

3. Local Event Sponsorships:
Sponsoring local events, fundraisers, or community gatherings can increase brand visibility and engagement within your local community. By associating your salon with positive community initiatives, you can enhance your reputation and build goodwill among local residents while also reaching potential clients who attend sponsored events.

Digital Marketing Tactics:

1. Social Media Marketing:
Establishing a presence on popular social media platforms such as Facebook, Instagram, and Pinterest allows you to connect with your target audience, showcase your nail art, and promote special offers or promotions. Social media platforms provide a powerful medium for visually showcasing your salon's services, sharing client testimonials, and engaging with followers through interactive content such as polls, contests, and live streams.

2. Email Marketing:
Building an email list of clients and prospects enables you to send regular newsletters, promotions, and updates to keep them engaged and informed about your salon. Email marketing allows you to personalize communication, segment your audience based on their preferences and behaviors, and drive repeat business through targeted promotions and offers.

3. Influencer Partnerships:
Collaborating with beauty influencers and bloggers in your local area or within your niche can help you reach a wider audience and

leverage their influence and credibility to promote your salon and services. Influencer partnerships allow you to tap into their engaged follower base, gain exposure to new potential clients, and generate buzz around your salon through sponsored content, reviews, and recommendations.

By incorporating a mix of traditional and digital marketing tactics into your overall marketing strategy, you can effectively reach your target audience, increase brand visibility, and drive client engagement for your nail salon. Experiment with different channels and tactics to identify what works best for your salon and adjust your approach accordingly to maximize results and achieve your marketing goals.

5. Incorporate Traditional and Digital Marketing Strategies:
   To maximize your salon's reach and effectiveness, consider incorporating both traditional and digital marketing strategies into your plan. Traditional marketing tactics can help you reach local audiences and establish a presence in your community, while digital marketing tactics can expand your reach beyond geographic boundaries and target specific demographics with precision. By leveraging a mix of traditional and digital marketing strategies, you can amplify your salon's visibility, attract new clients, and drive business growth.

In summary, a well-defined marketing strategy is essential for the success of your nail salon business. By identifying your target market, conducting market research, developing a marketing plan, and determining the appropriate marketing channels and tactics, you can effectively reach and engage with your target audience, differentiate your salon from competitors, and drive business growth in the competitive beauty industry landscape.

Building an Online Presence

In today's digital age, establishing a strong online presence is imperative for nail salons looking to attract clients and build brand awareness. Here's a detailed guide on how to create an impactful online presence:

1. Develop a Professional Website:

Start by creating a professional website that serves as the online hub for your nail salon. Your website should showcase your salon's services, pricing, location, contact information, and any special offers or promotions. Ensure that your website is visually appealing, easy to navigate, and mobile-responsive to provide a seamless experience for visitors. Incorporate high-quality images of your nail art and salon interiors to showcase your work and entice potential clients.

2. Optimize for Search Engines (SEO):

Optimize your website for search engines to improve its visibility and attract organic traffic. Conduct keyword research to identify relevant keywords and phrases that potential clients may use when searching for nail salon services online. Incorporate these keywords strategically into your website's content, meta tags, headings, and image alt text to improve your search engine rankings and increase your chances of being found by potential clients.

3. Establish a Presence on Social Media:

In addition to your website, establish a presence on popular social media platforms such as Facebook, Instagram, and Pinterest. These platforms provide valuable opportunities to showcase your nail art, connect with your audience, and promote your salon's services. Regularly post engaging content, such as photos and videos of your nail designs, behind-the-scenes glimpses of your salon, client testimonials, and special promotions. Use relevant hashtags and geotags to increase your visibility and reach on social media.

4. Engage with Followers:

Engage with your followers on social media by responding to comments, messages, and inquiries promptly. Encourage interaction by asking questions, running polls or contests, and soliciting feedback from your audience. Building genuine relationships with your followers helps foster loyalty and trust, ultimately leading to increased client retention and referrals.

5. Partner with Beauty Influencers and Bloggers:

Consider partnering with beauty influencers and bloggers to amplify your salon's reach and visibility. Identify influencers and bloggers whose audience aligns with your target demographic and reach out to them with collaboration proposals. Offer influencers complimentary nail services or exclusive discounts in exchange for social media posts, reviews, and mentions. Influencer partnerships can help increase brand awareness, credibility, and reach within your target audience, driving traffic to your salon and attracting new clients.

By following these strategies and leveraging the power of digital marketing, you can create a strong online presence for your nail salon, attract clients, and build lasting relationships with your audience in today's competitive beauty industry landscape.

Implementing Promotional Tactics

Promotional tactics play a crucial role in driving short-term sales and increasing client bookings for nail salons. Here's an in-depth exploration of effective promotional tactics and how they can benefit your business:

1. Introductory Offers:

Introductory offers are an excellent way to attract new clients and encourage them to try your salon for the first time. Offer discounted rates or complimentary services, such as a free manicure with a pedicure, to entice new clients to experience the quality of your services. Providing a positive first impression can lead to repeat business and referrals.

2. Referral Programs:

Referral programs leverage the power of word-of-mouth marketing by rewarding existing clients for referring new clients to your salon. Offer incentives such as discounts, free services, or gift cards to clients who refer friends, family members, or colleagues to your salon. Not only does this incentivize referrals, but it also helps strengthen client loyalty and trust in your brand.

3. Seasonal Promotions:

Capitalize on holidays, special occasions, and seasonal trends by creating themed promotions and nail art designs. Offer special packages or discounts for holiday-themed manicures or pedicures, such as Valentine's Day nail art or festive designs for Halloween. Seasonal promotions help generate excitement and attract clients looking to celebrate and indulge in themed nail services.

4. Loyalty Programs:

Implementing a loyalty program rewards clients for their loyalty and encourages repeat business. Offer incentives such as discounts, free services, or exclusive perks to clients who frequent your salon regularly. Consider implementing a points-based system where clients earn points for each visit or purchase, which can be redeemed for rewards or discounts on future services.

5. Limited-Time Offers:

Create a sense of urgency and encourage immediate action by offering limited-time promotions and flash sales. Promote exclusive discounts or special offers for a limited duration, such as a one-day flash sale or weekend promotion. Limited-time offers create a sense of urgency and FOMO (fear of missing out), motivating clients to book appointments and take advantage of the deal before it expires.

Tracking the effectiveness of your promotional tactics is essential for evaluating their impact and optimizing your marketing strategy. Monitor key metrics such as client acquisition cost, return on investment (ROI), and booking conversion rates to assess the success of your promotions. Use this data to refine your promotional efforts, allocate resources effectively, and maximize the impact of your marketing initiatives.

Implementing strategic promotional tactics can help drive short-term sales, increase client bookings, and foster client loyalty for your nail salon. By offering enticing promotions, tracking their effectiveness, and refining your approach based on data-driven insights, you can attract new clients, retain existing ones, and grow your salon business successfully.

In summary, developing a comprehensive marketing and promotion strategy is essential for building brand awareness, attracting clients, and driving business growth for your nail salon. By understanding your target market, building an online presence, and implementing effective promotional tactics, you can position your salon for success in the competitive beauty industry landscape.

Chapter 9:
Managing Operations Efficiently

Efficient management of operations is crucial for the smooth functioning and success of a nail salon. In this chapter, we will explore key aspects of managing operations efficiently, including scheduling and appointment management, inventory control, product management, bookkeeping, and financial management.

Scheduling and Appointment Management

Effective scheduling and appointment management are paramount for optimizing the productivity of your nail salon and delivering a seamless experience for clients. Here are some strategies to efficiently manage scheduling and appointments:

Investing in appointment scheduling software or salon management software can streamline the scheduling process and automate appointment bookings. Opt for a user-friendly platform that enables clients to book appointments online, view availability, and receive reminders via email or text message. By utilizing software, scheduling errors, double bookings, and missed appointments can be minimized, saving time for salon staff and enhancing client satisfaction.

Implementing block scheduling can enhance efficiency by allocating dedicated time slots for different types of nail services, such as manicures, pedicures, nail enhancements, and nail art. Organizing the schedule in blocks enables optimized staff utilization, reduces downtime between appointments, and ensures efficient use of salon resources. Consider factors like service duration, staff availability, and client preferences when structuring the schedule.

Maintaining flexibility in scheduling is essential to accommodate last-minute bookings, walk-in clients, and unforeseen changes or cancellations. By keeping a buffer in the schedule, you can account for unexpected delays or emergencies and adjust appointments as needed to accommodate client requests and preferences. Prioritizing exceptional customer service involves being responsive and accommodating to clients' scheduling needs.

Providing training to salon staff on effective appointment management techniques is crucial. Ensure that staff are proficient in using scheduling software, communicating with clients, and optimizing the appointment schedule. Additionally, they should be knowledgeable about service durations, booking policies, and salon protocols to facilitate smooth appointment transitions and minimize scheduling conflicts.

Implementing a system for confirming appointments and sending reminders to clients can help reduce no-shows and late cancellations. Send confirmation emails or text messages immediately upon booking appointments and follow up with reminder notifications closer to the appointment date. By doing so, appointment slots are utilized efficiently, and revenue loss for the salon is minimized.

By implementing these strategies, nail salon owners can streamline scheduling processes, optimize staff utilization, and enhance client satisfaction. Effective appointment management not only improves operational efficiency but also contributes to a positive salon experience for clients, ultimately leading to increased loyalty and business growth.

Inventory Control and Product Management

Proper inventory control and product management are essential for maintaining adequate stock levels, minimizing waste, and ensuring that the salon has the necessary supplies to meet client demand. Here are some strategies for managing inventory and products efficiently:

1. Inventory Tracking System: Implement an inventory tracking system to monitor stock levels, track product usage, and reorder supplies as needed. Use salon management software or inventory management tools to keep accurate records of inventory counts, product purchases, and supplier information. Regularly update inventory records and conduct physical counts to reconcile discrepancies and identify any issues or discrepancies.

2. Supplier Relationships: Cultivate strong relationships with suppliers and vendors to ensure timely delivery of products, competitive pricing, and reliable service. Research different suppliers and negotiate favorable terms, such as bulk discounts, flexible payment terms, and fast shipping options. Establish backup suppliers or alternative sources for critical products to mitigate supply chain risks and avoid disruptions to salon operations.

3. Product Selection and Merchandising: Curate a selection of high-quality nail products and brands that appeal to your target market and align with your salon's brand identity. Regularly review and update your product offerings based on client feedback, industry trends, and seasonal preferences. Display products prominently in the salon and utilize effective merchandising techniques to drive sales and encourage impulse purchases.

4. Inventory Optimization: Analyze inventory data and trends to identify opportunities for optimization and cost savings. Implement inventory control measures, such as establishing par levels, setting reorder points, and implementing FIFO (first in, first out) inventory management practices to minimize excess stock and reduce carrying costs. Utilize inventory reports and analytics to identify

slow-moving items, obsolete inventory, or areas for improvement in product selection and pricing.

5. Product Usage and Waste Reduction: Monitor product usage and consumption patterns to identify areas of waste or inefficiency. Train staff on proper product usage and handling techniques to minimize waste, spillage, and overuse. Consider implementing measures to reduce packaging waste, such as refilling bulk containers or using eco-friendly packaging materials. Implementing measures to reduce waste not only saves money but also contributes to environmental sustainability.

Bookkeeping and Financial Management

Effective bookkeeping and financial management are essential for maintaining the financial health and stability of your nail salon business. Here are some strategies for managing bookkeeping and finances efficiently:

1. Accounting Software: Invest in accounting software or salon management software with built-in accounting features to streamline financial record-keeping, invoicing, and reporting. Choose a user-friendly platform that integrates seamlessly with other salon management tools and allows you to track income, expenses, taxes, and profit margins accurately.

2. Separate Business and Personal Finances: Establish separate bank accounts and credit cards for your salon business to maintain clear separation between personal and business finances. Keep detailed records of all salon-related transactions, including income, expenses, purchases, and payroll, to facilitate accurate financial reporting and tax compliance.

3. Budgeting and Forecasting: Develop a budget and financial forecast for your nail salon to plan and allocate resources

effectively. Estimate anticipated revenues, expenses, and cash flow projections based on historical data, industry benchmarks, and market trends. Monitor actual performance against budgeted targets and adjust your financial plans as needed to stay on track and achieve your business goals.

4. Expense Management: Monitor and control salon expenses to minimize costs and maximize profitability. Review recurring expenses, such as rent, utilities, payroll, and supplies, to identify opportunities for cost-saving measures or efficiency improvements. Negotiate with suppliers for better pricing or terms, consolidate orders to take advantage of volume discounts, and implement cost-saving initiatives to optimize salon expenses.

5. Cash Flow Management: Maintain healthy cash flow by managing accounts receivable, accounts payable, and operating expenses effectively. Monitor cash flow regularly to ensure that there is sufficient liquidity to cover expenses, payroll, and other financial obligations. Implement strategies to accelerate cash inflows, such as offering incentives for prompt payments or implementing payment policies to reduce outstanding receivables.

6. Tax Planning and Compliance: Stay informed about tax obligations, regulations, and deadlines relevant to your nail salon business. Consult with a qualified accountant or tax advisor to develop a tax planning strategy and ensure compliance with local, state, and federal tax laws. Keep accurate records of income, expenses, deductions, and tax filings to minimize the risk of audits or penalties and maximize tax savings opportunities.

By implementing these strategies and best practices for managing operations efficiently, you can optimize the performance, productivity, and profitability of your nail salon business. Effective scheduling and appointment management, inventory control, product management, bookkeeping, and financial management are key components of a successful salon operation. By prioritizing operational excellence and adopting efficient management practices, you can enhance the client experience, minimize costs, and drive sustainable growth for your nail salon business.

Chapter 10:
Navigating Challenges and Overcoming Obstacles

Running a nail salon business comes with its own set of challenges and obstacles that owners must navigate to ensure success. In this chapter, we will explore the common challenges faced by nail salon owners, strategies for problem-solving and conflict resolution, and the importance of maintaining resilience and persistence in overcoming obstacles.

Common Challenges Faced by Nail Salon Owners

Competition:
One of the foremost challenges encountered by nail salon owners is the intense competition within the industry. With a plethora of salons competing for the attention of potential clients, distinguishing one's salon from the rest becomes imperative. Standing out amidst the competition necessitates a strategic approach encompassing unique branding, exceptional service offerings, and innovative marketing strategies. To effectively compete, salon owners must identify their unique value proposition and leverage it to attract and retain clients in a fiercely competitive market.

Staffing Issues:
Staffing issues, including recruiting and retaining qualified nail technicians, pose a significant challenge for nail salon owners. The search for skilled and dependable staff members can be arduous, compounded by the industry's high turnover rates. Staff turnover can disrupt salon operations, compromise service quality, and adversely impact client satisfaction. To address staffing challenges, salon owners must implement effective recruitment strategies, offer competitive compensation packages, provide ongoing training and development opportunities, and foster a supportive work environment conducive to employee retention.

Client Retention:
Maintaining client retention is paramount for the sustained success of a nail salon. In an environment characterized by fierce competition, nurturing client relationships and fostering loyalty is essential. Providing exceptional customer service, personalized experiences, and implementing loyalty rewards programs are instrumental in cultivating client loyalty and encouraging repeat business. By prioritizing client satisfaction and continually exceeding expectations, salon owners can foster long-term relationships with their clientele and drive sustainable growth.

Economic Factors:
Economic factors, such as fluctuating consumer spending habits, economic downturns, and inflation, pose formidable challenges for nail salon owners. During periods of economic uncertainty, consumers may exercise caution and reduce discretionary spending, leading to a decline in salon visits and revenue. To mitigate the impact of economic fluctuations, salon owners must develop resilience and adaptability, diversify revenue streams, and implement cost-effective strategies to maintain profitability during challenging economic conditions.

Regulatory Compliance:
Navigating regulatory compliance is a complex challenge faced by nail salon owners, who must adhere to various health, safety, licensing, and labor regulations. Failure to comply with regulatory requirements can result in fines, penalties, reputational damage, and legal repercussions, posing significant risks to the business. To ensure compliance, salon owners must stay abreast of regulatory changes, implement robust policies and procedures, provide comprehensive staff training on safety and sanitation practices, and conduct regular inspections to uphold industry standards and mitigate risks effectively.

While nail salon ownership offers numerous opportunities for growth and success, it also presents a myriad of challenges that must be navigated skillfully. By addressing common challenges such as competition, staffing issues, client retention, economic factors, and regulatory compliance, salon owners can position their businesses for long-term viability and prosperity in the competitive nail salon industry. Through strategic planning, effective management practices, and a commitment to excellence, salon owners can overcome obstacles and achieve sustainable growth and success in the dynamic and ever-evolving beauty industry.

Strategies for Problem-Solving and Conflict Resolution

Effective Communication:
Open and transparent communication serves as the cornerstone of a harmonious and productive salon environment. Encouraging staff to communicate openly with each other and with management about any concerns or challenges they may encounter fosters trust, collaboration, and problem-solving among team members. Establishing a culture of communication creates a supportive atmosphere where staff feel empowered to express their thoughts and ideas, leading to improved morale and job satisfaction. By facilitating effective communication channels, salon owners can address issues proactively, prevent misunderstandings, and cultivate a cohesive team environment.

Conflict Resolution Techniques:
Conflict is inevitable in any workplace, but how it is managed can make all the difference in maintaining a positive salon atmosphere. Developing conflict resolution techniques and protocols enables salon owners to address conflicts and disputes promptly and effectively. Encouraging staff to resolve conflicts constructively through active listening, empathy, and compromise promotes mutual understanding and fosters stronger relationships among

team members. Implementing formal procedures for conflict resolution, such as mediation or arbitration, provides a structured framework for resolving disputes and preventing escalation. By equipping staff with the tools and strategies to navigate conflicts professionally, salon owners can promote a culture of respect, cooperation, and mutual support within the salon.

Training and Development:
Investing in training and development programs is essential for empowering staff with the skills and knowledge they need to handle challenging situations effectively. Providing training on conflict resolution, customer service, and interpersonal communication equips staff with the confidence and competence to address issues professionally and diplomatically. Continuous learning and development opportunities not only enhance staff performance but also foster a culture of growth and resilience within the salon team. By investing in staff training and development, salon owners demonstrate their commitment to supporting employee growth and enhancing the overall quality of service delivery.

Positive Work Environment:
Creating a positive work environment is vital for fostering employee engagement, satisfaction, and retention. Recognizing and rewarding staff for their contributions, celebrating achievements, and fostering a sense of camaraderie and teamwork are essential elements of building a positive workplace culture. A supportive work environment where staff feel valued, respected, and supported encourages open communication, collaboration, and mutual respect. By prioritizing employee well-being and creating a positive salon atmosphere, salon owners can cultivate a motivated and cohesive team that is committed to delivering exceptional service to clients.

Seek External Support:
In some instances, seeking external support from HR consultants, business coaches, or industry associations can provide valuable insights and guidance in resolving complex issues or conflicts. External professionals bring impartial perspectives, facilitate constructive discussions, and offer practical solutions to address challenges effectively. Consulting with external experts allows salon owners to access specialized knowledge and expertise tailored to their unique circumstances, helping them navigate challenging situations with confidence and clarity. By leveraging external support, salon owners can gain valuable insights, develop effective strategies, and foster a supportive and resilient salon environment.

Maintaining Resilience and Persistence

Maintaining resilience and persistence is paramount for nail salon owners as they navigate the challenges inherent in running a successful business. Resilience, the ability to rebound from adversity, and persistence, the determination to pursue goals despite obstacles, are vital qualities in the competitive beauty industry. Here are some strategies for cultivating resilience and persistence:

Developing a Growth Mindset:
Cultivating a growth mindset is foundational to resilience and persistence. It involves reframing challenges as opportunities for growth and learning. By embracing setbacks as valuable experiences, salon owners can approach obstacles with optimism and a solution-oriented mindset. Viewing challenges as stepping stones rather than roadblocks fosters resilience and encourages continuous improvement.

Setting Realistic Goals:

Establishing clear, achievable goals provides direction and motivation for salon owners and their teams. Breaking down larger objectives into smaller, manageable tasks allows for steady progress and prevents overwhelm. By setting realistic goals and developing actionable plans, salon owners can maintain focus and momentum, even in the face of adversity.

Embracing Adaptability:
In the fast-paced beauty industry, adaptability is essential for responding to changing market dynamics and customer preferences. Salon owners must be willing to pivot, innovate, and adjust their strategies to meet evolving needs. Embracing adaptability allows salon owners to stay ahead of the curve, seize opportunities, and navigate challenges with resilience and agility.

Prioritizing Self-Care:
Maintaining resilience requires prioritizing self-care and well-being. Salon owners should carve out time for rest, relaxation, and rejuvenation to prevent burnout and sustain energy levels. Seeking support from friends, family, or professional networks can provide emotional reinforcement during challenging times. By prioritizing self-care, salon owners can recharge and replenish their resilience reserves.

Celebrating Progress:
Recognizing and celebrating progress, no matter how small, reinforces motivation and morale within the salon team. Celebrating achievements collectively fosters a positive and supportive salon culture, encouraging staff to persevere through obstacles. By acknowledging milestones and accomplishments, salon owners can inspire their team and cultivate a sense of pride in their work.

Building Support Networks:

Building a support network of mentors, peers, and industry professionals provides valuable guidance and encouragement. Networking with fellow salon owners allows for the exchange of ideas, experiences, and best practices. Leveraging support networks for emotional reinforcement and practical advice strengthens resilience and fosters a sense of community within the industry.

Maintaining Focus on the Long-Term Vision:
Staying focused on the salon's long-term vision and objectives is essential for sustaining motivation and resilience. Even amid short-term challenges, salon owners must keep sight of the bigger picture and remain committed to their goals. By maintaining a positive outlook and persevering through obstacles, salon owners can overcome adversity and realize their vision for success in the nail salon industry.

In conclusion, navigating challenges and overcoming obstacles is an inherent part of running a nail salon business. By recognizing common challenges, implementing effective problem-solving and conflict resolution strategies, and maintaining resilience and persistence, salon owners can overcome obstacles and achieve long-term success in the industry. By fostering a culture of collaboration, continuous learning, and adaptability, salon owners can build a thriving business that withstands challenges and flourishes in the face of adversity.

Chapter 11:
Growing Your Nail Salon Business

In the journey of running a nail salon, growth is not just desirable but often necessary for long-term success. As a nail salon owner, expanding your business goes beyond just increasing profits; it involves enhancing customer satisfaction, staying ahead of competition, and establishing a sustainable business model. In this chapter, we will explore various strategies and tactics for growing your nail salon business, focusing on expanding your services and offerings, increasing revenue streams, and scaling your operations for long-term success.

Expanding Your Services and Offerings

As a nail salon owner, expanding your services and offerings is a strategic approach to attract new clients, retain existing ones, and increase revenue streams. In today's competitive market, offering a diverse range of services is essential to cater to the varied preferences of customers and maintain a competitive edge. By introducing additional nail care services beyond traditional manicures and pedicures, you can create opportunities to upsell and cross-sell, thus increasing revenue and customer satisfaction.

One avenue for expansion is to introduce spa treatments to your service menu. Spa treatments such as hand and foot massages, exfoliation, and moisturizing treatments add a luxurious and pampering element to the nail salon experience. These services not only provide relaxation and rejuvenation but also enhance the overall perceived value of your salon, attracting clients seeking a comprehensive spa-like experience.

Another option is to offer specialized treatments aimed at addressing specific nail concerns or preferences. For example, nail strengthening treatments can cater to clients with weak or brittle nails, while nail repair services can target those with damaged or broken nails. By addressing common nail issues and providing solutions, you can position your salon as a trusted provider of holistic nail care services.

Additionally, consider incorporating nail art workshops or classes into your offerings to tap into the growing trend of DIY nail art enthusiasts. Hosting workshops where clients can learn basic nail art techniques or participate in themed nail art events can create a sense of community and engagement, fostering loyalty and repeat business. Moreover, offering specialized training sessions for aspiring nail technicians can serve as a unique selling point and attract individuals interested in pursuing a career in the beauty industry.

Expanding your service menu not only caters to a broader range of customer preferences but also positions your salon as a one-stop destination for all nail care needs. By offering a comprehensive range of services, you can encourage clients to spend more time and money at your salon, thereby increasing revenue per visit and enhancing customer lifetime value. Furthermore, a diverse service menu can differentiate your salon from competitors and attract clients seeking a more personalized and immersive nail salon experience.

In conclusion, expanding your services and offerings as a nail salon owner is a strategic approach to attract new clients, retain existing ones, and increase revenue streams. By diversifying your service menu to include spa treatments, specialized nail care services, and nail art workshops, you can cater to a broader range of customer preferences and enhance the overall customer experience. Moreover, offering a comprehensive range of services positions your salon as a one-stop destination for all nail care needs, fostering customer loyalty and generating repeat business in the competitive beauty industry.

Increasing Revenue Streams

In addition to expanding your nail salon services, exploring additional revenue streams is a proactive strategy to foster business growth and enhance profitability. By diversifying your income sources, you can mitigate risks, increase revenue potential, and adapt to changing market dynamics. Here are some effective ways to explore additional revenue streams for your nail salon:

1. Retail Products:
Consider offering retail products such as nail polishes, nail care kits, or beauty accessories for sale to clients. Retail sales not only provide an additional revenue stream but also offer clients the convenience of purchasing professional-grade products for at-home use. Stocking high-quality products that complement your salon services can enhance the overall customer experience and encourage repeat purchases.

2. Collaborative Partnerships:
Explore partnerships with complementary businesses such as hair salons, spas, or beauty boutiques to cross-promote services and attract new clientele. Collaborative partnerships allow you to leverage each other's customer base, expertise, and resources to mutual benefit. For example, you could offer joint promotions or package deals with a nearby hair salon, where clients receive discounts for booking services at both establishments. Collaborative partnerships can expand your reach, increase brand visibility, and drive revenue growth through shared marketing efforts and referral networks.

3. Online Sales:

In today's digital age, online sales present a lucrative opportunity for expanding your revenue streams. Consider selling nail care products, accessories, or gift certificates through your salon's website or online marketplace platforms. Online sales enable you to reach a broader audience beyond your local area, tap into new markets, and capitalize on the growing trend of e-commerce. Additionally, offering online booking services can streamline the appointment scheduling process for clients, enhancing convenience and accessibility.

4. Subscription Services:
Subscription services are another innovative way to diversify revenue streams and foster customer loyalty. Consider offering subscription boxes or membership programs where clients receive curated nail care products, exclusive discounts, or VIP perks on a recurring basis. Subscription services provide a predictable stream of revenue and encourage repeat business by offering ongoing value and incentives for clients to remain engaged with your salon.

5. Mobile Nail Salon Services:
Explore opportunities for diversifying revenue streams through mobile nail salon services, catering to clients' evolving needs and preferences. Mobile nail salon services involve offering on-site nail care services at clients' homes, offices, or events, providing convenience and flexibility for busy individuals. By offering mobile services, you can reach clients who may prefer the privacy and convenience of receiving nail treatments in their preferred location, thereby expanding your customer base and revenue potential.

In conclusion, exploring additional revenue streams beyond traditional salon services is a proactive approach to growing your nail salon business and enhancing profitability. By offering retail products, forming collaborative partnerships, leveraging online sales channels, implementing subscription services, and exploring mobile nail salon services, you can diversify income sources, attract new clients, and adapt to changing market trends. By embracing innovation and creativity in your revenue generation strategies, you can position your nail salon for sustained success and long-term growth in the competitive beauty industry.

Scaling Your Business for Long-Term Success

Scaling your nail salon business involves a strategic approach to expanding operations while maintaining quality, profitability, and customer satisfaction. It requires careful planning, investment in resources, and a focus on sustainable growth strategies. Here are some key steps to scale your nail salon business effectively:

1. Assess Current Business Model:
Begin by evaluating your current business model, infrastructure, and resources to identify areas for improvement and expansion. Assess factors such as service offerings, pricing structure, target market, operational processes, and staffing requirements. Identify any bottlenecks or inefficiencies that may hinder growth and develop strategies to address them.

2. Invest in Technology Solutions:
Consider investing in technology solutions to streamline salon operations, enhance efficiency, and improve the overall customer experience. Implement salon management software to automate appointment scheduling, manage inventory, and track client information. Utilize online booking systems to allow clients to book appointments conveniently through your website or mobile app. Incorporate customer relationship management (CRM) tools to manage client relationships, track preferences, and personalize marketing communications. Embracing technology can streamline administrative tasks, free up staff time, and enhance the salon's professionalism and efficiency.

3. Build a Strong Team:
Focus on building a strong team of skilled and motivated staff who share your vision and values. Invest in recruiting, training, and retaining talented nail technicians, receptionists, and support staff who are passionate about delivering exceptional service. Empower your team with ongoing training and development opportunities to enhance their skills and keep them motivated. A cohesive and dedicated team is essential for maintaining quality service standards, fostering a positive work culture, and driving business growth.

4. Maintain Quality and Consistency:
As your salon expands, prioritize maintaining high standards of quality, consistency, and professionalism across all aspects of your business. Ensure that all staff members are trained and equipped to deliver consistent, high-quality nail care services that exceed customer expectations. Implement quality control measures, regular performance evaluations, and customer feedback mechanisms to monitor and maintain service quality. Consistency is key to building trust, retaining customers, and sustaining long-term success in the competitive beauty industry.

5. Develop Strategic Marketing Initiatives:
Develop strategic marketing and branding initiatives to increase brand awareness, attract new clients, and retain existing ones. Utilize a mix of online and offline marketing channels to reach your target audience effectively. Leverage social media platforms, email marketing campaigns, influencer partnerships, and local advertising to promote your salon and showcase your services. Develop a strong brand identity, unique selling proposition (USP), and brand messaging that resonates with your target market. Implement customer loyalty programs, referral incentives, and

promotional offers to reward loyal customers and encourage repeat business.

6. Implement Scalable Growth Strategies:
Implement scalable growth strategies that allow your nail salon to expand gradually while maintaining profitability and sustainability. Consider opening additional salon locations in strategic locations to reach new markets and expand your customer base. Explore opportunities for diversifying revenue streams, such as retail product sales, collaborative partnerships, subscription services, or mobile nail salon services. Continuously monitor key performance indicators (KPIs), track financial metrics, and adjust your growth strategies as needed to ensure long-term success and profitability.

In conclusion, scaling your nail salon business requires a strategic approach that encompasses investments in technology, team building, quality control, marketing, and scalable growth strategies. By implementing these key steps, you can position your salon for long-term success, sustainability, and profitability in the competitive beauty industry.

In conclusion, growing your nail salon business requires a strategic approach that involves expanding services and offerings, exploring new revenue streams, and scaling operations for long-term success. By diversifying services, increasing revenue streams, and scaling operations effectively, you can attract new clients, enhance customer satisfaction, and drive business growth in the dynamic and competitive beauty industry.

Conclusion

Embarking on the journey of starting and managing a nail salon is a rewarding endeavor filled with challenges, triumphs, and endless opportunities for growth. Throughout this comprehensive guide, we've delved into every aspect of establishing and running a successful nail salon business, from crafting your vision and navigating legal considerations to marketing your services and managing operations efficiently.

As a nail salon owner, you play a pivotal role in shaping the beauty industry landscape, providing clients with a sanctuary where they can express their creativity, enhance their appearance, and indulge in self-care. By leveraging your unique vision, passion for nail care, and commitment to excellence, you have the power to create a salon experience that resonates with clients, fosters loyalty, and sets your business apart from the competition.

As you celebrate your achievements and look ahead to the journey that lies ahead, remember to stay resilient in the face of challenges, embrace innovation and adaptability, and cultivate a positive work culture that empowers your team and delights your clients. With dedication, perseverance, and a spirit of creativity, there is no limit to what you can achieve in the dynamic and ever-evolving world of nail care.

In closing, I offer you these final words of encouragement as you continue your journey as a nail salon owner. Remember that entrepreneurship is a journey filled with ups and downs, successes and setbacks, but it's also a journey of growth, learning, and fulfillment.

Stay resilient in the face of challenges, persevere in pursuit of your goals, and maintain a positive attitude even in the face of adversity.

Surround yourself with a supportive network of mentors, peers, and industry professionals who can offer guidance, advice, and encouragement along the way.

Above all, never lose sight of your passion for nail care and your commitment to providing exceptional service to your clients. Your dedication, creativity, and passion are the driving forces behind your success, and they will continue to fuel your journey as you strive for excellence in the nail salon industry.

With determination, perseverance, and a spirit of innovation, the possibilities for your nail salon business are limitless. As you embark on the next chapter of your entrepreneurial journey, I wish you continued success, fulfillment, and prosperity in all your endeavors.

Whether you're just starting out on your entrepreneurial journey or seeking to take your existing salon to new heights, I hope this guide has provided you with valuable insights, inspiration, and practical strategies to guide you along the way. As you embark on this exciting adventure, I wish you success, fulfillment, and prosperity in all your endeavors. Here's to the continued growth and success of your nail salon business!

www.ingramcontent.com/pod-product-compliance
Lightning Source LLC
Chambersburg PA
CBHW070353230526
45471CB00006B/2545